The For

2007

The Forward book of poetry
2007

FORWARD
LONDON

First published in Great Britain by
Forward Ltd · 84–86 Regent Street · London W1B 5DD
in association with
Faber and Faber · 3 Queen Square · London WC1N 3AU

ISBN 0 571 23448 8 (paperback)

Reprographics by Wyndeham Icon
Printed by CPI Bath
Lower Bristol Road · Bath BA2 3BL · UK

A CIP catalogue reference for this book
is available at the British Library.

To Ghazi

Preface

UNBELIEVABLY, fifteen years have passed since we announced the very first Forward Poetry Prizes. In that year Thom Gunn won Best Collection, Simon Armitage Best First Collection and Jackie Kay Best Single Poem. Stealing from Longfellow when he wrote 'Art is long, and Time is fleeting', I would say that time is fleeting but art is long: the years may inexorably slip though our fingers but poetry stays with us, the best influencing and inspiring each new generation. It is wonderful to see, alongside a great master of the art like the Nobel laureate Seamus Heaney, that we have several contenders in this year's shortlists who were not even born when he was winning his first prizes for published poetry. The fact that about half a century separates the oldest from the youngest represented in this year's *Forward book of poetry* is surely a sign not only that poetry continues to flourish but that poets, as well as their work, endure and go from strength to strength.

The task of singling out the best from the merely excellent is never an easy one, and I applaud the judges – John Burnside in the chair, with Moniza Alvi, Sam Leith and Sebastian Faulks – for their decision in this particularly rich and fruitful year to nominate six poets in each of the shortlisted categories rather than the more usual five. I would like to thank each of them for their acuity, dedication and goodwill.

As always, I am grateful to the many individuals behind the scenes: Felix Dennis for his continued support; to our partners in promoting poetry: Jules Mann and The Poetry Society, Gary McKeone and Arts Council England, Faber and Faber, the BBC and the Colman Getty team, including Dotti Irving, Liz Sich, Kate Wright-Morris and Truda Spruyt, and everyone at Forward.

William Sieghart

Foreword

If there is one thing I have noticed over the last few years, it is that there never seems to be enough time to read all the books I would most like to read. Part of this is purely personal, but mostly it indicates a trend that, for someone of my generation, is rather surprising. A child of the Sixties, I grew up believing that technology would rescue me from the more routine tasks of the day to day, leaving me free to learn the flute, practise my rock climbing and – most important of all – spend long and fruitful hours reading. I'm not at all sure what went wrong between the first promise of 'labour-saving devices' and now, when everyone seems, in spite of our admirable technology, so much more rushed and – in the worst possible way – preoccupied. But if there is one luxury that being a judge of a competition like the Forward offers, it is the opportunity simply to sit down and read, with the attention good writing deserves.

This year's published poetry has offered a fine vintage, as this anthology of poems by both emerging talents and established voices will, I hope, prove. And so the task of singling out the year's best, both in collections and as single poems published in journals and magazines, has been a more than usually difficult one.

What has made that task, for me, more pleasurable and less guilt-ridden than it might have been, has been the companionship of my fellow judges. They brought to our initial meeting, and to the discussions that followed, a sense of the enjoyment of poetry, the responsibilities of judgement and a determination to listen carefully to the views of others, and to respond with a degree of commitment and understanding that, in my own experience, has never been equalled. All of us – Moniza Alvi, Sam Leith, Sebastian Faulks and myself, as chair – brought passion and engagement to the table but, as a judging team, we were looking for a near-magical consensus and, as elusive as such things often are, I do believe we found it. Our shortlist for Best Collection included work by a Nobel Prize winner, a second book by a fairly new poet, and volumes by two former winners of the Forward Best First Collection. Our shortlists for Best First Collection and Best Single Poem are, I believe, as diverse and as engaging as it is possible to be. At the time of writing, no winners have been decided, and there are no foregone conclusions (we are comparing collections, not careers) but I do feel confident of a satisfying outcome.

This is not to say that fine collections have not been omitted from our lists. This really has been an exceptional year for poetry, and it proved very hard to stick to the limits with which we began the process – so much so, indeed, that for both the Best Collection and Best First Collection categories, we extended the shortlist to six, rather than the more usual five. The outcome, I think, not only honours the work of the year's most interesting collections, but also showcases the richness and diversity of poetry that is being published in Britain today.

Of course, the problem for most of us is finding time to read them all. I hope this anthology will prove valuable to the general – that is, to the otherwise preoccupied – reader. In an age when time for close reading is hard to come by, and when so many other forms of writing are so much more visible – in bookshops, in the media – I hope it will also provide a reminder of the deep and lasting satisfaction to be gained from reading poetry. When time is short, what could be more appropriate, or more enjoyable, than a poem, so brief on the page, and so rich to the ear, so memorable in its music, and so subtle in its re-imagining of a world we so often take for granted. Poetry renews the world, renews the way we experience life, in ways that other writing cannot quite reach. So: take a break; sit back; read. In an age of busyness and needless hurry, nothing could be more nourishing to body, mind and soul.

John Burnside, *July 2006*

Publisher acknowledgements

John Agard · True Grit · The Blond Sheep in the Family · Subliminally Yours · *We Brits* · Bloodaxe Books

Simon Armitage · Evening · *Tyrannosaurus Rex Versus the Corduroy Kid* · Faber and Faber

Kate Bingham · Monogamy · Divorce · *Quicksand Beach* · Seren

Billy Collins · I Ask You · *The Trouble With Poetry and Other Poems* · Picador

Allan Crosbie · Manifesto · *Outswimming the Eruption* · The Rialto

Kwame Dawes · Legend · *Impossible Flying* · Peepal Tree

Patricia Debney · Welsh Poppy · *How to Be a Dragonfly* · Smith/Doorstop Books

Imtiaz Dharker · Its Face · *The Terrorist at My Table* · Bloodaxe Books

Jasmine Donahaye · Faith · *Missappropriations* · Parthian

Tishani Doshi · The Deliverer · Turning Into Men Again · *Countries of the Body* · Aark Arts

Stephen Dunn · The House Was Quiet · *The Insistence of Beauty* · WW Norton and Company

Jane Duran · To My Mother and Father · *Coastal* · Enitharmon Press

Paul Farley · Automatic Doors · The Heron · *Tramp in Flames* · Picador

Vicki Feaver · Glow-Worm · The Gun · *The Book of Blood* · Jonathan Cape

Roderick Ford · Giuseppe · *The Shop*

Caroline Gilfillan · The Painter · *Poetry News*

Bill Greenwell · Absent Fathers · Keeping Fit with Jesse James · *Impossible Objects* · Cinnamon Press

Ian Gregson · Freeze Frame · A Coypu · *Call Centre Love Song* · Salt Publishing

Vona Groake · The Undercurrent · *Juniper Street* · Gallery Books

Philip Gross · *from* The Assembled · *The Egg of Zero* · Bloodaxe Books

John Hartley Williams · Requiem for a Princess · *London Review of Books*

Dennis Haskell · Sydney or the Bush · *all the time in the world* · Salt Publishing

Seamus Heaney · The Harrow-Pin · The Blackbird of Glanmore · *District and Circle* · Faber and Faber

W N Herbert · Cove Park · *Bad Shaman Blues* · Bloodaxe Books
Tobias Hill · From the Diaries of Henry Morgan, Summer 1653 · *Nocturne in Chrome & Sunset Yellow* · Salt Publishing
Gaia Holmes · Claustrophobia · *dr james graham's celestial bed* · Comma Poetry
John Kinsella · Against Conflation · *The New Arcadia* · WW Norton and Company
John Kinsella Forest Encomia of the South-West · *Poetry Review*
Tim Liardet · The Language School · *The Blood Choir* · Seren
Andrew McNeillie · In Memoriam Carey Morris RA (1882–1968) · *Slower* · Carcanet Press
Valeria Melchioretto · Cubism · *Ambit*
Peter Morgan · 'Warum, Warum...?' · *August Light* · Arc Publications
Togara Muzanenhamo · Captain of the Lighthouse · *Spirit Brides* · Carcanet Press
Sean O'Brien · Fantasia on a Theme of James Wright · *Poetry Review*
Caitríona O'Reilly · A Qing Dish · *The Sea Cabinet* · Bloodaxe Books
Jacob Polley · The Cheapjack · *Poetry London*
Peter Reading · *from* -273.15 · *-273.15* · Bloodaxe Books
Robin Robertson · La Stanza Delle Mosche · Lizard · *Swithering* · Picador
Jane Routh · The Red Cow · *Teach Yourself Mapmaking* · Smith/Doorstop Books
Anne Ryland · *from* The Island's Bride · Blue Shadows · *Autumnologist* · Arrowhead Press
Fiona Sampson · Trumpeldor Beach · *The Wolf*
Clare Shaw · Bird · *Straight Ahead* · Bloodaxe Books
Penelope Shuttle · Bashō · Six-Billionth Baby · *Redgrove's Wife* · Bloodaxe Books
Ruth Silcock · The Perils of Ageing · *Biographies etc* · Anvil Press Poetry
Ivan Silverberg · The Equine Encounter · Obsessed With Pipework
Charles Tomlinson · The Portuguese Ox · *Cracks in the Universe* · Oxford Poets/Carcanet Press
Tim Turnbull · Goodbye Yellow Brick Road · Whoops · *Stranded in Sub-Atomica* · Donut Press
Chase Twichell · Cocktail Music · *Dog Language* · Bloodaxe Books

Susan Utting · WOODWORK · *House Without Walls* · Two Rivers Press
A Van Jordan · IN SERVICE · *M.A.C.N.O.L.I.A.*
WW Norton and Company
Jane Weir · CIGAR · *The Way I Dressed During the Revolution* ·
Templar Poetry
Tim Wells · BEN SHERMAN · ON BEING EXPELLED FROM ETON FOR SHAGGING TALLULAH BANKHEAD · *Boys' Night Out in the Afternoon* ·
Donut Press
Hugo Williams · WALK OUT TO WINTER · *Dear Room* · Faber and Faber
Michael Arnold Williams · BLAENAFON BLUE · *Poetry Wales*

Contents

Shortlisted Poems – The Forward Prize for Best Collection

Shortlisted Poems – The Felix Dennis Prize for Best First Collection

Shortlisted Poems – The Forward Prize for Best Single Poem

Highly Commended Poems 2006

Shortlisted Poems
The Forward Prize for Best Collection

Kate Bingham

Monogamy

I blame it on the backlash: free love
in the Eighties was for hippies, no one
liked Thatcher but monogamy
seemed more efficient, comforting to State
and individual alike, less last
resort than a celebration in bed

of the right to choose, not make your bed
and lie in it so much as a labour of love
we willingly fell in with, certain at last:
I wanted you, you wanted me. Alone
for the first time and in no fit state
for company we didn't see monogamy –

dumb, satisfied, unsung monogamy –
sneak in and slide between us on the bed,
backdating itself as if to reinstate
respectability, disguised as love's
romantic ideal and mocking our offhand, one
night stand bravado. It wants us to last,

our happiness, like a disease, its last
chance to spread – as if monogamy
transmits non-sexually from one
adoring couple to the next – to embed
itself in a world where pleasure and love
live separately and sit again in state,

pass sentence on what neither Church nor State
condemn outright. But what if we do last?
Time's not the test. Who loves best won't always love
longest, might not respect monogamy's
insistence, its assumption that all beds
must be forsaken but the one

one lies in in love. My eyes are for no one
but you, my love. We lie in a state
of easy innocence, a bed
of roses, tumbled and fragrant to the last
linen bud, but what's monogamy
without temptation, faith without love?

Therefore for love we should sacrifice one
thing alone: monogamy; maintain a state
of mutual jealousy, outlast our bed.

Divorce

I had been looking forward to divorce –
recriminations, therapy and casual sex,
the disentangling of my life from yours

by sympathetic girl solicitors
who blush referring to you as my ex
and practice to avoid their own divorce.

I would have let you keep the chest of drawers
and hung my pants and socks on picture hooks
like bunting. What was mine would be not yours,

I'd cut my hair (too short) make common cause
with spinsters in wine-bars, bandy regrets
or shrug them off: you marry, death or divorce

come next, or so I thought. But love endures –
the mirror in the wardrobe door reflects
your face in mine and mine in yours,

a couple of fond baggy shameless bores
blessed with unmitigated happiness.
At night I wake from dreaming of divorce,
my arms and legs in sweat, tangled with yours.

Paul Farley

The Heron

One of the most begrudging avian take-offs
is the heron's 'fucking hell, all right, all right,
I'll go the garage for your fucking fags'
cranky departure, though once they're up
their flight can be extravagant. I watched
one big spender climb the thermal staircase,
a calorific waterspout of frogs
and sticklebacks, the undercarriage down
and trailing. Seen from antiquity
you gain the Icarus thing; seen from my childhood
that cursing man sets out for Superkings,
though the heron cares for neither as it struggles
into its wings then soars sunwards and throws
its huge overcoat across the earth.

Automatic Doors

When I see some kids springing the gallery doors
I lament the great revolvers. As we enter
a new era of doors, I can remember
the thrill involved, the stately, dumb inertia

at first, before they'd give, a slow surrender
to four heaving kids, storing our power,
a glass and darkwood turbine; how whatever
effort we put in, the doors would answer

as they gathered speed, until only a shoulder
nudge was needed (and though no passengers
were carried, sometimes I'd grab the bar
and dangle in my quadrant). We'd spin for hours

or so it seemed: we were time travellers
fast forwarding ourselves into the future
before we were thrown out, into an era
of never even having to lift a finger.

Vicki Feaver

Glow-Worm

Talking about the chemical changes
that make a body in love shine,
or even, for months, immune to illness,
you pick a grub from the lawn
and let it lie on your palm – glowing
like the emerald-burning butt
of a cigarette.

                    (We still haven't touched,
only lain side by side
the half stories of our half lives.)

You call them lightning bugs
from the way the males gather in clouds
and simultaneously flash.

This is the female, fat from a diet
of liquefied snails, at the stage in her cycle
when she hardly eats; when all her energy's
directed to drawing water and oxygen
to a layer of luciferin.

Wingless, wordless,
in a flagrant and luminous bid
to resist the pull to death, she lifts
her shining green abdomen
to signal *yes yes yes*.

The Gun

Bringing a gun into a house
changes it.

You lay it on the kitchen table,
stretched out like something dead
itself: the grainy polished wood stock
jutting over the edge,
the long metal barrel
casting a grey shadow
on the green-checked cloth.

At first it's just practice:
perforating tins
dangling on orange string
from trees in the garden.
Then a rabbit shot
clean through the head.

Soon the fridge fills with creatures
that have run and flown.
Your hands reek of gun oil
and entrails. You trample
fur and feathers. There's a spring
in your step; your eyes gleam
like when sex was fresh.

A gun brings a house alive.

I join in the cooking: jointing
and slicing, stirring and tasting –
excited as if the King of Death
had arrived to feast, stalking
out of winter woods,
his black mouth
sprouting golden crocuses.

Seamus Heaney

The Harrow-Pin

We'd be told, 'If you don't behave
There'll be nothing in your Christmas stocking for you
But an old kale stalk.' And we would believe him.

But if kale meant admonition, a harrow pin
Was correction's veriest unit.
Head-banged spike, forged fang, a true dead ringer

Out of a harder time, it was a stake
He'd drive through aspiration and pretence
For our instruction.

Let there once be any talk of decoration,
A shelf for knick-knacks, a picture-hook or -rail,
And the retort was instant: 'Drive a harrow-pin.'

Brute-forced, rusted, haphazardly set pins
From harrows wrecked by horse-power over stones
Lodged in the stable wall and on them hung

Horses' collars lined with sweat-veined ticking,
Old cobwebbed reins and hames and eye-patched
  winkers,
The tackle of the mighty, simple dead.

Out there, in musts of bedding cut with piss
He put all to the test. Inside, in the house,
Ungulled, irreconcilable

And horse-sensed as the travelled Gulliver,
What virtue he approved (and would assay)
Was in hammered iron.

The Blackbird of Glanmore

On the grass when I arrive,
Filling the stillness with life,
But ready to scare off
At the very first wrong move.
In the ivy when I leave.

It's you, blackbird, I love.

I park, pause, take heed.
Breathe. Just breathe and sit
And lines I once translated
Come back: 'I want away
To the house of death, to my father

Under the low clay roof.'

And I think of one gone to him,
A little stillness dancer –
Haunter-son, lost brother –
Cavorting through the yard,
So glad to see me home,

My homesick first term over.

And think of a neighbour's words
Long after the accident:
'Yon bird on the shed roof,
Up on the ridge for weeks –
I said nothing at the time

But I never liked yon bird.'

The automatic lock
Clunks shut, the blackbird's panic
Is shortlived, for a second
I've a bird's eye view of myself,
A shadow on raked gravel

In front of my house of life.

Hedge-hop, I am absolute
For you, your ready talkback,
Your each stand-offish comeback,
Your picky, nervy goldbeak –
On the grass when I arrive,

In the ivy when I leave.

Robin Robertson

La Stanza Delle Mosche

The room sizzles in the morning sun;
a tinnitus of flies at the bright windows,
butting and dunting the glass. One dings
off the light, to the floor, vibrating blackly,
pittering against the wall before taxi
and take-off – another low moaning flight,
another fruitless stab at the world outside.
They drop on my desk, my hands,
and spin their long deaths on their backs
on the white tiles, first one way
then the other, tiny humming tops that
stop and start: a sputter of bad wiring,
whining to be stubbed out.

Lizard

Volatile hybrid of dinosaur and toy, this
living remnant throbs on the hot stone:
a prehistoric offcut, six inches
of chlorophyll-green dusted with pollen;
a trick of nature – lithe, ectopic, cuneiform –
a stocking-filler, out of place everywhere
but in the sun. Frisking the wall,
its snatched run is a dotted line
of fits and starts, spasmodic, end-stopped.
It pulses once; slips into a rock with a gulp.

Penelope Shuttle

Bashō

Bashō
saw the birth of a fawn
on the birthday of the Buddha,

omen of such an auspicious nature
he had to spend
the rest of his life living it down.

On his last journey,
when spring came
he sold his winter clothes,

just as my daughter did,
three hundred years later,
as she travelled not in Japan

but north to south
down the long pounding heart of China.

Six-Billionth Baby

Today sees the birth of the world's six-billionth baby.
By the time he's an old man

the car-parking nightmare of Falmouth
will be resolved

and I will be long-gone.

By the time the six-billionth baby
is an elderly ex-millionaire

or a one-time mayor of Bombay,
I'll be experiencing non-being.

Maybe the afterlife
will be disappointing as a cloudy eclipse
or unjust as the death of the Cornish tongue,

maybe lovely and ungrudging
as in my life
only your daughterhood shone.

Shortlisted Poems
The Felix Dennis Prize for Best First Collection

Tishani Doshi

The Deliverer

Our Lady of the Light Convent, Kerala

The sister here is telling my mother
How she came to collect children
Because they were crippled or dark or girls.

Found naked in the streets,
Covered in garbage, stuffed in bags,
Abandoned at their doorstep.

One of them was dug up by a dog,
Thinking the head barely poking above the ground
Was bone or wood, something to chew.

This is the one my mother will bring.

*

Milwaukee Airport, USA

The parents wait at the gates.
They are American so they know about ceremony
And tradition, about doing things right.

They haven't seen or touched her yet.
Don't know of her fetish for plucking hair off hands,
Or how her mother tried to bury her.

But they are crying.
We couldn't stop crying, my mother said,
Feeling the strangeness of her empty arms.

*

This girl grows up on video tapes,
Sees how she's passed from woman
To woman. She returns to twilight corners.

To the day of her birth,
How it happens in some desolate hut
Outside village boundaries

Where mothers go to squeeze out life,
Watch body slither out from body,

Feel for penis or no penis,
Toss the baby to the heap of others,

Trudge home to lie down for their men again.

Turning into Men Again

This morning men are returning to the world,
Waiting on the sides of blackened pavements
For a rickshaw to carry them away
On the sharp pins and soles of their dancing feet.

They must go to the houses of their childhoods
To be soothed. They must wait for the wheels
To appear from the thin arm of road.
They must catch the crack in the sky

Where the light shifts from light to dark
To light again, like the body in the first stages of love;
Angering, heightening, spreading:
Bent knees, bent breath.

Now they are moving, changing colours.
Women are standing at the thresholds of doors
Holding jars of oil, buckets of hot water and salt,
Calamine, crushed mint and drink.

Some crawl into their mother's laps,
Collapse against the heavy bosoms of old nannies,
Search for the girl who climbed with them
To the tin roof for the first time.

Inside, in the shadows of pillars,
Fathers and grandfathers are stepping down
From picture frames with secrets on their lips,
Calling the lost in from their voyages.

Bill Greenwell

Absent Fathers

Absent fathers stand in parks,
cupping their smokes like cuckoo-spit
and watching the swings fly high.

Their eyes lie flat against their heads,
taking evasive inaction.

In winter, when the children go,
and roundabouts are frozen sick,
they clap themselves mechanically
and study their watches.

When they missed the rehearsal,
they found themselves without a line
or even a squint of the limelight:

they are walk-ons, extras.
In their chafed faces, you can still see
the silhouettes of intention,

before the absence, and before
the daily pilgrimage to the child's slide.

Keeping Fit with Jesse James

Each afternoon he exercised... he scraped his sweat off with a butter knife – Ron Hansen

In corpore sano.
Rides himself bareback,
lets his body bathe in sweat,
soaks himself up like applause, stands,
bends horseshoes straight with his hands.

Bruises his palms
as the flashing axe pulps the good wood.
Under the sunlight, suspenders down,
whirls two yellow pins
in a blur of arcs, and begins

to glister. Holsters
hang low. Muscles pumping,
jumps the surrey up from a squat
nineteen times, preens. Out of doors
the butter melts, golden, from his pores.

Dunks his fresh head
in the horse's bucket. His son,
six, is hunched on his honeyed shoulders.
Toes snag the garter snakes
gently. Whatever it takes.

Ian Gregson

Freeze Frame

A household is threatened by forces that could open it up.
        A tannoy echoed in the living-room
Of a couple I knew, whose house looked down on trains and
        platforms.
        It unnerved me like a homely showroom,
Warm light on armchairs, serried lounges, all in a windy field.
        Perhaps the pressures rose then forced a change.
Lamplight had shone behind the curtains which embayed it like
        Their intimacy and the walls, but then
Maybe it had started to feel provisional –
        A shelter somehow not complete; rising,
Destinations prised a way through the furniture.
        Through a door left open I stumble
Detective-like into a frame isolated from a plot.
        On the table is a disappointed lead
Coiled towards its kettle, and leaves where he must have split
        The coupled tea bags. One of them had said
You're walling me in, for through a quarter circle
        Back and forward an erect umbrella rocks
On its pins, and I can hear two strangers in the bathroom –
        Conversation drifted there in the wind.
What ought to be inward was prised open, until they were
        Cohabiting with North Atlantic moods.
Their thoughts linger head-high above the pine-table, tangled
        As the flight-paths of a cloud of midges.
A cold front has spread from the kitchen. Causes tangle
        With symptoms; onions nude in vinegar
Jarred and smarting shudder on their old refrigerator
        That palpitates and wheezes, pumping its breath
Into a flat frozen in the puzzled look of a photograph
        Its subjects have vacated. Two stiffs

Are clasped together in the teapot like a couple in lava.
        Leavers and arrivers are embarrassed:
High above the platform the lit casement is uncurtained,
        Exposing its hurt interior to the dark.

A Coypu

Lovers between them can make
another mind whose ideas
neither apart would conceive
resembling *folie a deux*
as wishes resemble fears.

Lovers together even see
differently from each apart,
or so I thought after that walk
between the fenced-in marsh and the shore:
that creature hurried from you and me

down a line we wrote together –
neither of us could be sole author
both of its strong claws and its webbed feet.
Interacting we assembled
this tubby, furry other

pulling a tail like an afterthought.
I started as though from the danger
of what we'd make of one another
if my wishes conspired with yours.
The couple we are is a stranger

like the bright owl we must've made up
ghosting from the trees into a brief
tiff with a crow, then off through the park
a thousand miles south of its range
like stories we invent jointly that return
as memories, and haunt belief.

Anne Ryland

From The Island's Bride

vi Sea Script

One vast page ranging away from view,
   no paragraphs for pauses. Where to begin,
how to find a loose thread that invites
   unravelling. Each sentence slips out of
its predecessor and into the next, wave
   upon wave of calligraphy, not a lapse or
hesitation in sight. This is a complex
   and perfect grammar, and I always loved
a verb table, the way tenses string
   together as pearls, each mirroring another,
and those cupboards a linguist builds
   in her mind, where accusative, dative,
genitive are stored for instant access,
   the carved drawers of etymology, where
tide derives from *time*. Later, I may
   evolve into marine lexicographer, a creature
of the shore, gathering and annexing
   the sea's textures, until I become bilingual
in its liquid language. But for now
   I must learn the words as a child does,
like braille, tracing them by finger
   in the sand, the slow kinaesthetic method.
My first letter is the shape of a small
   purse, or is it a lip, just slightly open.

Blue Shadows
after 'Woman with a Ewer' by Johannes Vermeer

After the redness of dawn
has melted away,
the morning light explores
flakes and abrasions on the wall.
I allow it to follow the arc of my arm
and rinse the inner places
water will never reach.
A moment repeats itself indefinitely.
Rooms relax in their shadows,
doors open and close
as if whispering.
Hand on the window,
I am mesmerized
by the geometry of each glass pane:
let these blues filter through white
and crisp planes of linen.
Mine is a pale life of small tasks.
It is not what I had in mind.

Tim Turnbull

Goodbye Yellow Brick Road

We vault over the barrier and scramble
down the bank. Our boots are soaked with dew,
our clothes spattered with mud and torn by brambles.
The headlights leach the battery as the bonnet
spews out steam. The car will stay there, slewed
and stuck, up on the verge, till traffic cops
find time to slap a Police Aware sign on it
and, later, send a truck to haul it off.

There'll be no search. Nobody knows we're gone.
A trawl of Swansea's all they can afford.
Staff levels as they are, they'll just send forms
to flop among the circulars and bills
and get thrown out. We're strictly off the record,
left no forwarding address, unencumbered
by possessions, heading, nameless, for the hills.
Erased, rubbed out, we are not even numbers.

We avoid the roads, return to the farm
and find that it's a ruin. The animals
have fled to the edges of the wood. The barn
is wrecked, its roof caved in. Disconsolate,
the cattle bawl, reluctantly feral.
We skirt the village, weave across an orchard,
pop a window, steal dry socks and chocolate,
make tea and toast and leave by the back yard.

The moor's awash with shifting cloud. I take
your red, raw hands. Your face is beautiful.
Your cheeks are pink. It is too cold to speak.
We've got the gun and nearly forty rounds
and food and know we are invulnerable –
that nothing matters now, or can go wrong.
The whip of wind, footsteps in sodden ground,
the blistering rain. This is our love song.

Whoops

The beer makes him talkative
and weepy.
He clutches Caroline's
chubby fingers in his own
calloused paws

and tells her
how much he still loves her;
how, in truth,
she was the only girl,
and there had been many,
the only girl
he ever really loved.
She gives a weak smile,
having heard it all
a thousand times before.

A table away, his bride
of three months,
the girl he brought here
from New Zealand,
looks on, damp-eyed
and slack-jawed.

A grand piano topples
from a skyscraper window.
The old pit shaft opens
under the weight of the horse.

Tim Wells

Ben Sherman

In the 70s, people thought the future
would be flyless suits and hoverpacks.
I knew it would be no change really,
drunken yobs in Ben Shermans
kicking the shit out of each other.
Feels good to have backed a winner.

On Being Expelled from Eton for Shagging Tallulah Bankhead

I never went to Eton,
Nor shagged any Hollywood sirens.
But if I'd had the background
And the privileges that money provides,
Then I'd have been there, mate.
Been there, pink gin in one hand, dick in the other.
The 1920s were made for a bloke like me.
Brilliantine, lady air pioneers, bobbed hair, and Mack Sennett.
The decade that roared.
I've read nearly all of Fitzgerald, even *The Vegetable*.
I'd have fitted right in.
Me, Timothy George Wells, Esquire.
A lost generation, groping its way in the dark.
Oh, Tallulah,
A girl who, reputedly, bedded forty per cent of British aristocracy.
British, not English.
That's a lot of nobs.
We're talking proper bad girls here.
Bad girls with a sense of class.
Alabama girls thrown out of daddy's house for "immoral proclivities."
Girls discovering sex, drink, parties, and fabulous frocks.
Ah, that I was a feckless aristocrat
With an absurd moniker
And an even more ridiculous nickname,
Motoring to the Hotel de Paris on a sunny summer morn
With the star of *Thirty a Week*.
She throws the car round a bend,

One hand on the wheel, t'other on my thigh,
Eyes on my Petronious.
I nervously quip a saucy epigram from Martial.
She nuzzles my ear and whispers,
"I've been called many things, but never an intellectual."
Oh my dear, does it require an academic to teach the facts of life?
The First Lord of the Admiralty, William Bridgeman no less,
MI5, the Home Office,
All concerned for our morals.
But us lads at Eton are dining out on our salad days.
This scandal, like me, will be sat on.
Seduced by the girl as pure as the driven slush.
She's always skating on thin ice
And everyone wants to be there when it breaks.
My grandfather watched her films.
He died coughing black lung in the 1990s.
Tallulah's last words...
"Codeine! Bourbon!"
My only regret is the playboy life
I never had...
On being expelled from Eton for shagging Tallulah Bankhead.
Well, it's better than Spanish flu, coal mining, the General Strike,
And what my family really did through the 1920s.

Shortlisted Poems
The Forward Prize for Best Single Poem
in memory of Michael Donaghy

John Hartley Williams

Requiem for a Princess

(i)

A penguin, a donkey, a piano.
Their tinkle-plonky grief.

A station trolley
rumbling over pavement slabs
carries the deceased.

Black hearse, black iceberg
in a warm dissolving ocean,
it sails toward the gulf
that it will occupy.

The flag is folded small,
the folding of a child. Smoothed
from the national laundry
is a crease.

The penguin. Its raised beak.
Its self-important air. An advice bird.

Rising trumpets lift up
through shafts of attic sunlight.
Sound-motes. The air is soothed.
Chords on dusty keys.

There she goes!
Straight as a die!

Tantara!

(ii)

A press of the old
against the young, craning
their necks to watch
the sombre rigadoon.

More friends she had
than secret yellows on a wasp,
ghosting
the popular tune.

The shouts of a sergeant-major
wheel the regiment.
What are the thoughts of a serving man?
Tender? Insolent?

Their black trousers
are striped with gold.

(iii)

Here is the man in the stovepipe hat
who is writing this poem.

Surreptitiously,
a pouch of verses round his neck,
he has joined the procession
astride a donkey.

Downward

into the bone
of her creaturely self

he is melting,
against his will...

(iv)

Ever see, the penguin remarks, *so many poems, candles...?*
The donkey twitches its ear.
Don't happen to play the piano, by any chance? the penguin asks.
The donkey twitches its ear.

A little hoof clatter
on the ivories?
A jig? A reel? A little bonzo
up-and-at-'em stomp?

Donkey fixes penguin
with long, donkey regard.

We need a melody
sweet as it is clumsy.
We need a song
that does it with its thumb...

Donkey moves to piano stool,
places feet upon the keys.

Yeah! cries the penguin.
Hoof it, Jack!

(v)

Becoming audible somewhere
is ragtime, hot & strong...

But do not assume
because you can hear
what you can hear
that it is other than

axes to the splinters
of a sounding board.

At rigid attention,
the penguin
stands absolutely straight
for a piano-smashing song...

Synch your lips
to words without reprise.

(vi)

On a 94 bus, a donkey.
Wossat? asks a passenger.
Never seen no donkey before? the conductor asks.
Not on a bus, says the passenger.
Well you have now, says the conductor.
He checks the traveller's season,
who alights, subsequently, at the junction
of Goldhawk Road & King Street.
That a piano I hear? asks the passenger.
Not on my bus, the conductor yells.

Everyone on board
wishes they would stop.

(vii)

Alice wilds the pack.
The donkey does not move.

Court cards blown
across a wiry back

snow it out of grey.
Where the donkey stands,

argent on a field, fesse,
heraldry becomes the land,

a colourful finesse
of King, Queen, Jack

or floral coat of arms
ushering the fade to black.

Wolves look up from their bones.
Flowers ruffle to a night-breeze.

A ray of moonlight
striking the face of an owl

catches in its wasp-eyed gaze
reflection of the slow disband

of mourners clutching discards,
… hers… his… these…

John Kinsella

Forest Encomia of the South-West

I

Head State Forester, my grandfather
surveyed jarrah and counted pines
tucked into the hardwood
as soft sell, short shrift,
quick-growing
turnarounds; watched fire
sweep across his fiefdom,
crosscut into ledgers,
health of that jarrah and marri,
blackbutt on the fringe,
named the fastidiousness
of his Scottish wife
Ann Livy Plurabelle,
and made her Irish
where the convolution of sounds
was called "the bush", and dances
at Jarrahdale were as far
away as the hospital.

Kinsella is a road and a forest.
Kinsella is an overlay.
Kinsella is a post-war boom-time
verging on the changing ways.
He died when I was a few years old.
He smoked heavily.
Was tall with a parched face.
My father took me to look at the absent signifier,
the hollow birth-right. The fire-tower,
the ever-ready batteries' cardboard cylinders
still below, the phone smashed by vandals.
Up the fire trail, on the granite summit,

hard-core partying place.
Arsonist incidentals' irony
too good to refuse as the lighter gloats
in high temperature and fuck, man, you've set it off,
can't stamp it out, let's get the fuck out of here.
They don't say a word, ever. But you've
met them in pubs. You've seen the spark
in their eyes, their hatred of forests.

The resinous hardwood I split with an axe
as if under the seared surface
it's seamed;
                    from a young age the off-cuts
of his bush upbringing – my father, his father –
where he chopped the finger
off a cousin – a dare on the chopping block –
my father. His father walloped him.

The family from County Wicklow,
foresters there,
foresters here,
a man's man…
and you're Claude's
grandson?
Surprising.

2
Reportage? When
they came in at Ludlow
they cut the massive open-forest tuarts
and tried farming. That's the 1850s
and there's little talk
of Nyungar people in the forest,
though an artist tells me
there are Kinsellas who are blackfellas,
and I wonder why I've never met them,

heard of them. I want to find them,
for them to find me.

The sand-mining company
has the government in its pocket – this
is a barely renovated cliché –
and in the forest, police,
saying they'd be over the line
along with the dreadlocks and guitars
if the law told them to,
said all you can do
is watch the survey markers.
I ring lawyers. If they go outside
the allotted space... indigenous rights,
rare species, all are collated
in the effort to resist. Failure
allots expediency to the roadside camp
and issues of masculinity: locked on,
boys score points and tally arrests,
the forests goes under, girls
in dungarees call on the moon goddess,
and they move on.

3
My father, long separated from the forests
of his birth, drives through the wooded country
just for the sake of driving. I like to go up
into the hills, he says. Just to drive.

4
Surrounded by the paraphernalia of foresting
the cutting and tearing of bark is head over shoulder
in the pit, raining down flaky tears,
an electric rip – of the tongue,
taste not so unlike the taste we have of ourselves,
skin, flesh, chapels in a clearing,

wound sucked dry,
ice-skimmed water baptismally broken,
threads of mist as sunrises and sunsets
suffused are as much as we witness
on open plains, oceans;
never mind the pain
of working bullocks.

5
Giving the finger to a logging truck
is giving the finger to small-town rage
against heritage imagined as consistency
and moral equilibrium, as connection,
as vacant spaces grind logic into woodchips
and the spout shoots out time sheets.

Giving the finger to a logging truck
is to make the barrelled weight of trunks shift
against the squared U-prongs of praise, offerings-up,
gimleted throats to chain and separate
from the better halves of self; in the blood,
the rush is a drink in a bar that trucks no ferals.

Giving the finger to a logging truck
is a shooting offence, and a get-busted for dope-
carrying offence, and a laying-open of the secret
places retribution comeback getting ahead
making a buck fuck the old-growth lock-up
pent-up release, the swerve of the big wheel

ratio to asphalt and hitch-hiker
stranger danger fallout.

6
Mettle and impulse are group settlement
nano-probe Borg cube homesteads

rendering karri stands fused with paper
the good word is printed on,
anaphora in keeping accounts.
So lengthy the cordage,
building the State,
O liberty looked out upon
from the tall trees.

7

Sustainable equals dispossession.
Sustainable equals clear-felling.
Sustainable equals selective picking out of infrastructure.
Sustainable equals dieback.
Sustainable equals balance of payments.
Sustainable equals nice floorboards in parliamentary metonymics.
Go where you want with this.
Sustainable equals God at the top of the pyramid, logging
companies the next rung down.
Sustainable equals the wood for the trees.
Sustainable equals the log in your eye, the splinter in your sister's.
Sustainable equals ochre rivers and a peeling-back of the layers
of allegory – extended metaphors all the way to the sea.
Sustainable equals the widened highway and its support services'
flow-on effect.
Sustainable equals the commiserating blocks on the forest's edge
reaching into the forest bit by bit with the
environmentally-minded eroding their privilege bit by bit.
Sustainable equals the forest-loving dope-grower who crushes the
micro with every step, as delicate and caring as they might
be, introducing weeds as s/he never would with prickly
pear or rose, the rabbits loving the tender shoots, O
children of nature.
Sustainable equals dieback trod and trod through by effusing
bushwalkers infiltrated by bird calls – shocked into
spirituality by the weather calls of white-tailed black
cockatoos.

Sustainable equals stars cut out around milling towns, forming the
southern cross in nation-building recognition of later
migrant influence.
Sustainable equals forest by any other name.
Sustainable equals election promises come up trumps, couched in
reassurances.

8
It's so wet in there: wetter
than anywhere else. A deflected wet
that intensifies, gets under all cover.
In the ice cold you sweat,
and are we under the layers,
the canopy focussing
hard-hitting echoes
on every pore,
clasping undergrowth
too succulent, luring
you in where it's no drier.

9
Extra-wide gravel roads
deep south so fire won't roll
as smoke so dense
you crawl
slower than through the worst fog
tightened windows preventing
not of the suffocating sting
you associate with those
you love most, love most
in the time left to you,
the pluming crown of flame
as much a vision
as you're going to get.

Sean O'Brien

Fantasia on a Theme of James Wright

There are miners still
In the underground rivers
Of West Moor and Palmersville.

There are guttering cap-lamps bound up in the roots
Where the coal is beginning again.
They are sinking slowly further

In between the shiftless seams,
To black pools in the bed of the world.
In their long home the miners are labouring still –

Gargling dust, going down in good order,
Their black-braided banners aloft,
Into flooding and firedamp, there to inherit

Once more the tiny corridors of the immense estate
They line with prints of Hedley's *Coming Home*.
We hardly hear of them.

There are the faint reports of spent economies,
Explosions in the ocean floor,
The thud of iron doors sealed once for all

On prayers and lamentation,
On pragmatism and the long noyade
Of a class which dreamed itself

Immortalized by want if nothing else.
The singing of the dead inside the earth
Is like the friction of great stones, or like the rush

Of water into newly opened darkness. Oh my brothers,
The living will never persuade them
That matters are otherwise, history done.

Jacob Polley

The Cheapjack

What do I have for as near as damn it?
What do I sell but I'm giving away?
  Might I pick my own pockets
  and slit my own throat
and dump myself dead in a shop doorway?

Daffodils, bird whistles, bobble hats,
fickle fish, slinkies, your name spelled in wire;
  caterpillars, mouse mats,
  trick plastic dog-shit,
conniptions, predictions and God's own fire.

I've bargained myself to Bedlam and back,
and a wonder it is that I'm not less flesh,
  for I'd sell you the scraps,
  the loose skin, the slack,
the tips of my toes and the last of my breath,

and might as well for the good my breath's done;
I've blown suits, jobs, marriages, houses and lands:
  I'm a man overcome
  by his profligate tongue,
and if you get close, you can stand where I stand.

What'll it cost? Not as much as you think.
What have you got? That'll do. Here's my nod,
  here's my wink,
  here's my blood for the ink.
I'm begging you now: my life for the lot.

Fiona Sampson

Trumpeldor Beach

Glimmering and vast
– Matthew Arnold

Beside you, water breaks brightly
on sand –
a rhythmic
exhalation
then the delicate downward raking
through a scree of shells;

salt-blisters bloom between your toes
like the blossom of foam

gathering,
dissolving
the edge of pure glare
silked here
with ocean pink and blue.
Through each pale colour
you can almost see light
itself:

filamented waves, each pulling a dot of pigment
up to the brink of your eye
and back,
a continual to and fro
of smudge
and reflection –

your glimpsed lash
like a small fault in the view,
the shadow of your
self

falling through the sky's
expanded lens.

Now spool back
down this sequence of markers – self, lash –
to the molecule
trembling on the brink of becoming
you:

it hangs inside you,
moment by moment
its painstakingness
millions of years old.

Bracelets of molecules
forming gleaming filaments and bubbles
out of thin air,
as mysterious to you
as to the applauding light;

and this flushes through you
like a change in temperature –
the understanding
that you are at the mercy of chains
and chambers
of water:

*

they float in the membrane,
mercurial. Adhering,
shifting –
you're occluded one moment,
the next
open
to biting molecules of air;
challenge

and relinquishment.
                    One moment after another
taking you up
                    and dropping you
as if there can be no rest
for this splay-fingered bodily apparatus
doggedly deliquescing
and refiguring
                    (mucus, blush,
pressure on a kidney);
the machinery
                    with which you convert water to light,
daily miraculous –
each eye.

*

Standing in smart clothes, holding your shoes clear,
you make the sea a radiant screen

sometimes suffused with shivers, or stretched
tight as skin

over itself.
It screens the beach-room

you've inhabited since childhood,
that's built against your ear.

Easy to exchange an elephant-hide Atlantic
for the mercurial Med,
                    this dazzler

whose urgent narratives from the middle of the world
are slurring up against your bare feet –

a salad of old rope,
coke-tins, the parted armaments of bivalves.

From the cafés
comes the smell of onions frying

as if the vivid sea itself
were burning them;
the fold and collapse of water,

like a hundred deckchairs,
a cheerful lie

that laps the ear's membrane.

Water
always pressing towards water

as if it could dissolve the skin of the known world
into droplets.

*

The modern city
tremoring against the early-morning sky,
sending itself upward in delicate
white flames behind you,
is hallucination.

It shifts in light
the way water
shifts a gleam from place to place –
the silk surface sly as story,
a myth
in which water combusts.

These are the fictional angels,
these bursts of supra-natural radiance
you could put your hand through;
that melt
                at the shadow of your foot
when you try to step in
to accept their cold
brilliant baptism.

                                Coins of shadow
shift in the pebbled water;
                                        tipped, balanced.
Always this intermingling
as if of strands within streams
rolling over each other, stone over stone
rounded on each other
                                        but indissoluble –

in the valves and ventricles of your own body
shadow
            and deep red luminescence;

the ghost of another country
rolling against light,
                                    among the shipping lanes,

floating towards some notional horizon –
a slur of light on water.

Michael Arnold Williams

Blaenafon Blue

She's taking those blue robes again,
the cowl, the cloak, her sensible shoes,
And yes, she's finding the old bike, too,
The high one, with the place at the front,
for her Gladstone bag,
With those awful devices of glass,
vermilion rubber, pie-dish enamel.

I can feel myself shrinking, already younger, smaller,
only a youth, a boy with ankle socks,
Four years out on the ice, three in the garden
with her big forearm raised.
Only one, and then, inside, but just a half of me,
An egg of the ovary that's supposed to sign off.
Poor old Dad, he'll get it wrong again.

I'm with her now, out from Sirhowy, up from Ebbw,
over Nantbwch and into Forge Side,
On past Pwll Mawr,
and we're flying down Mary Street,
Cornflower blue skirts out, like a sand yacht.

But heavy stuff; she's sweating below her corsets.
They're all in labour round at Rifle Green.
Everyone's howling,
Even the husbands, even the mothers,
even the mothers-in-law.
The doctor's done on Port Wine, and he can't come,
But the basket hanging on the front,
that's filled with raw meat;
It's the afterbirths from all the wives of Blaenafon.

Here, gently, pop one in the fire,
it'll fry a bit, but never mind.
You can chuck some more in the river.
Gently in marinades of rust
they'll slip on down past Varteg, towards Ponty,
And out then, to the tides,
Or submarine,
hidden below the slick-surfaced waters they'll go,
Like slack medusae in the moonlight.

And then there's the fathers.
One out of ten can't pass, or he's got small coal,
grit in the urethra.

Did you ever see a glass catheter?
Well, the male urethra is about six inches,
and they're no bigger in Blaenafon than anywhere else.
You've seen the crook of the thing?
You just have to twist that slightly, to get connection.
And what a relief!

We're celebrating filling the pisspots in Blaenafon.
But don't worry,
It's all for boys with one short leg here,
all down hill,
They'll get this lot below, at Pontnewynydd, or Aber,
or at Llantarnam, by the biscuit works;
Ten million eaten every day.

And in any case, Mother swears that this stream,
the Torfaen,
Is rattling full already, with kidney calc and molars,
all the gallstones of those old iron workers,
God help them,
And no harm so far, no harm at all.

Highly Commended Poems

2006

John Agard

True Grit

Here comes a black Englishman with a brolly.
To forget either would indeed be folly.

The Blond Sheep in the Family

John Bull Junior, not quite a chip off the old block.
Did one educate him to be a blond dreadlock?

Subliminally Yours

Our subconscious feeds on a subcontinent's spices
Even while munching Mr Kipling's almond slices.

Simon Armitage

Evening

You're twelve. Thirteen at most.
You're leaving the house by the back door.
There's still time. You've promised
not to be long, not to go far.

One day you'll learn the names of the trees.
You fork left under the ridge,
pick up the bridleway between two streams.
Here is Wool Clough. Here is Royd Edge.

The peak still lit by sun. But
evening. Evening overtakes you up the slope.
Dusk walks its fingers up the knuckles of your spine.
Turn on your heel. Back home

your child sleeps in her bed, too big for a cot.
Your wife makes and mends under the light.
You're sorry. You thought
it was early. How did it get so late?

Billy Collins

I Ask You

What scene would I rather be enveloped in
than this one,
an ordinary night at the kitchen table,
at ease in a box of floral wallpaper,
white cabinets full of glass,
the telephone silent,
a pen tilted back in my hand?

It gives me time to think
about the leaves gathering in corners,
lichen greening the high gray rocks,
and the world sailing on beyond the dunes –
huge, oceangoing, history bubbling in its wake.

Outside of this room
there is nothing that I need,
not a job that would allow me to row to work,
or a coffee-colored Aston Martin DB4
with cracked green leather seats.

No, it is all right here,
the clear ovals of a glass of water,
a small crate of oranges, a book on Stalin,
an odd snarling fish in a frame on the wall,
and these three candles,
each a different height, singing in perfect harmony.

So forgive me
if I lower my head and listen
to the short bass candle as he takes a solo
while my heart
thrums under my shirt –
frog at the edge of a pond –
and my thoughts fly off to a province
composed of one enormous sky
and about a million empty branches.

Allan Crosbie

Manifesto

Our patience will not yield, our resolve will not break.
We will liberate our children's minds.
We will protect their innocent hearts.
Our strong actions will follow our strong words.
The thirsty will drink, the hungry will eat.
We will teach you to believe what you read.

We will teach you to believe what you read.
Our patience will not yield, our resolve will not break.
The thirsty will drink, the hungry will eat.
We will liberate our children's minds.
Our strong actions will follow our strong words.
We will protect their innocent hearts.

We will protect your innocent hearts.
You will learn to believe what you read.
Strong actions will follow these strong words.
Our patience will not yield, our resolve will not break.
We will liberate our children's minds.
The thirsty will drink, the hungry will eat.

The hungry are drunk, the thirsty may eat.
We will not betray their innocent hearts.
We will not enslave our children's minds.
They will never disbelieve what they read.
Our patience will not yield, our resolve will not break.
Strong actions first demand strong words.

Strong actions first demand strong words
like, *If the thirsty drink and the hungry eat*
our patience will not yield, our resolve will not break.
We will not betray the innocent heart
of this manifesto – believe what you read.
Read my lips: we will enslave your children's minds.

To free them, we must enslave your children's minds.
The actions of the strong speak louder than their words –
if you refuse to believe what you read,
the thirsty won't drink, the hungry won't eat.
We will protect our innocent hearts.
We have patience. You will suffer, yield, break.

We will read your hungry minds.
We will break your strong, strong hearts.
You will eat our innocent words.

Kwame Dawes

Legend
For Kojovi

A deep pink face webbed in canary-yellow netting,
swaddled in infant finery – flesh soft to the eye.
This is how we first met; you, unblinking,

a week old, and the order of my life shifted.
I was four and you seemed outside of me,
outside of meaning. The nine months before

were blank, no recollection of waiting
for what must have been our mother's
marvellously round body. For it to turn

to this. At four, I stared at the full-length
mirror, then sprinted to the back of it
to find my revenant. My first inexplicable

equation: the hide-and-seek of my image.
How easily it slipped away. At four,
all was accommodation of mysteries, a new baby

the advent of snails after rain, the wide
valley of guinea-pig grass – a green, fluent sea
on which our cement and glass house sailed;

the magic appearance and disappearance
of this man, Neville, our father who grinned
while bearing you like he did gifts

from exotic ports; smiling proudly
with that familiar gap-tooth and mischievous
eyes gray as a blind man's marble eye;

bearing you, his lump of pink flesh,
eyes tightly shut, fingers curled.
Now the world had changed as worlds must.

Patricia Debney

Welsh Poppy

for Molly

Here you are, rushing in again at the last minute, settling where you will. From a distance I could confuse you with the others lining the road in bright yellow spring. But of course you are a delicate flower, no staid daffodil or trenchant dandelion. I can see as I get closer that you will always be young, your hat always blowing, half-covering your face now caught in laughter, your hand half up to hold it on.

Imtiaz Dharker

Its Face

A woman getting on a plane.
This is how it will happen.
A bird that has stopped singing
on a still road. This is how it will sound.

This cloth belongs to my face.
Who pulled it off?

That day I saw you
as if a window had broken.
Sharp, with edges that could cut
through cloth and skin.

You wrapped my mouth in plastic
and told me to breathe in free air.
This is how it will feel.

I remember heroes.
Figs, dates, a mango.
This food, your enemy's food.
This is how it will taste.

It will not come
slouching out of the ground.
It walks along a street
that has a familiar name.

This is how it will look.
It will have my face.

Jasmine Donahaye

Faith

After the rain, the Jehovah's Witnesses return.
One, that dark, blue-eyed woman, wears
immaculate politeness like an ironed raincoat.
On the doors to the left and the right of mine
the signs that read *No Proselytizing* act

as a kind of bait. I have tried anger,
the claim of other faiths, petty rudeness.
I tear open the door raving, but they always come back.
These women walk so slowly: they have
all the time in the world; they have such utter calm.

After they've gone I go out to weed
the wet garden and touch the grass roots
glistening with mud. On every leaf
there's a tongue of water, and the rosemary
leans her porcupine body against me, shivering.

Stephen Dunn

The House Was Quiet
After Stevens

The house was quiet and the world vicious,
peopled as it is with those deprived
of this or that necessity, and with weasels, too,
and brutes, who don't even need
a good excuse. The house was quiet as if it knew
it had been split. There was a sullenness
in its quiet. A hurt. The house was us.
It wasn't a vicious house, not yet. We hadn't
yet denuded its walls, rolled up its rugs.
It had no knowledge of the world
and thus of those who, in the name of justice,
would ransack belongings, cut throats.
Once the house had resounded with stories.
Now it was quiet, it was terrible how quiet it was.
And, sensing an advantage, the world pressed in.

Jane Duran

To My Mother and Father

I miss you as if you were fiction
and the ink still wet
where we crossed paths –

as if I invented you backwards
with the steam train, the tight grass, downpour,
old solutions I hold to my heart

as my boy holds his coat to his chest
before he puts it on.
I am still trying to understand you.

You become inextricable from Manhattan,
New Hampshire, Martha's Vineyard,
the last reflective windows, uptown din,

the Henry Hudson Parkway,
how many sad entries to the city.
I miss you as if nothing were lost

but only articulated.
And I dream about you.
I pull myself up by my roots.

Roderick Ford

Giuseppe

My Uncle Giuseppe told me
that in Sicily in World War Two,
in the courtyard behind the aquarium,
where the bougainvillea grows so well,
the only captive mermaid in the world
was butchered on the dry and dusty ground
by a doctor, a fishmonger, and certain others.

She, it, had never learned to speak
because she was simple, or so they'd said.
But the priest who held one of her hands
while her throat was cut,
said she was only a fish, and fish can't speak.
But she screamed like a woman in terrible fear.

And when they took a ripe golden roe
from her side, the doctor said
this was proof she was just a fish
and anyway an egg is not a child,
but refused when some was offered to him.

Then they put her head and her hands
in a box for burial
and someone tried to take her wedding ring,
but the others stopped him,
and the ring stayed put.

The rest they cooked and fed to the troops.
They said a large fish had been found on the beach.

Starvation forgives men many things,
my uncle, the aquarium keeper, said,
but couldn't look me in the eye,
for which I thank God.

Caroline Gilfillan

The Painter

Mopping his face, the painter accepts
vodka, pickles, speckled sausage.
Climbs the stairs to prop his easel
in four windowfuls of light, where he

sits, paint sluggish on palette,
drugged by syrup slip of birdsong,
watching nurse maids shoosh prams
like black sows up and down the road.

This man in smock and scarlet cravat
can't know that Warsaw will be drilled
to stumps, that the villa will swallow
families shorn to bone, dragging

in hand-carts a grandmother's table, a trunk,
bentwood chairs skittered down a staircase,
a set of engraved *herbata* glasses
knotted in a scarf with shaking fingers.

This man with turpentine tickling his nose
can't know that a husband and wife will remain
in their single room, the children dispersed,
the woman in overall and wrinkled socks,

the man thick-fisted, hitched to braces,
rasping the path with a twig broom,
staring as we curse the mosquitoes. Brag about
amber, silver. Plan cheap flights home.

Vona Groake

The Undercurrent

Anywhere. So long as there's a flicker of sea,
a far-fetched train, a lighthouse nodding off
between tea-time and that moment when
your father brightly takes you by the hand
to a place that is the opposite of home.
'Not over the rocks in darkness, Paddy.
You don't mean to tell me that.'

Philip Gross

From The Assembled

2

Friends... Quite what the word meant then
        escapes me. We had them:
    names our parents would learn
to ask after, and might never meet.

Did we talk? About what? We had so little
        history in us – the one
    family each, which was the only
one, ever, in the world, so what's to say?

In place of life stories, we had hobbies,
        sticking in, making lists
    and saving things so insignificant
I can't remember what mine were – only,

somewhere in the process, was the bleak
        exhilaration of having
    got, at last, the *whole set of*...
what? Who cared? It was something to be.

Dennis Haskell

Sydney or the Bush

1

I walked the wide streets of Billabigola
seeking an ATM;
I'd as well have searched for a whale in cola
spouting hysterical phlegm, a
cappuccino strip, boutiques or a sale of vertical rhyme,
a kibbutz, a blitz, or a train arriving on time.

2

But only crows now stalk the old captains' walk,
the bowling greens are brown,
the pavement's splitting, and the train's a bus
that lurches from a distant town.

3

Nothing's high but the petrol prices
and the yellowing sun, that graces
the one-eucalypt, uncut park
and its abject Aboriginal faces.

4

All future and sky seem to be blowing astray
the pioneers' ideals flying
from this once historical ground; here
"heritage" is a synonym for "dying".

5

The bank is gone, the church is dead, the only
things buzzing are flies
that flap and flop, too tired to fly
through country and western skies.

6

Each voice knows the other, name and initial.
A story's a story, and just proves
endless, where every word runs ritual;
each tongue hardly moves
even in stress: change can be glacial
and every flash of grammar is facial.

7

They're city lights' diet: scenic Australian towns
where the streets are hysterically quiet;
the scones are staling, the few shops failing,
and all the present is memory.

W N Herbert

Cove Park
for Polly and Julian

The rain would like to make us all Chinese.
I climb the hill with my umbrella fanned,
through bracken drooping like a sleeve's brocade
where hands with long quartz nails have been withdrawn.
My feet are fussy as a scholar's clogs
as I traverse the wire-suspended bridge:
two studded planks above the thickened burn
that imitates a southern love song heard
last night, and all the grasses wave the pearls
they've caught in their sharp tentacles. I stop
and look back at the loch, the dark felt hills
beyond: a centipede of mist crawls down
and, waving its antennae, starts to cross
the water, while a rainbow's banner hangs
from trees, and on Loch Long the character
for 'submarine' tears paper in its wake.

Tobias Hill

From the Diaries of Henry Morgan, Summer 1653

And so on May Day's eve I came to London,
with John Twentyman still riding beside me,
still chastising London even as we entered her,
her great steeples rising northwards and everywhere
bells, like those of towns in certain stories,
arisen from the sea on just such nights as these.

A dour and good man John Twentyman seemed,
and prudish in all he said, remarking
that the country life is much to be preferred,
there being Works of God there, and herein
nothing that has not been touched
into its present form by the hands of men;
but I have heard poor word of him since then,
and think the less of him for his hypocrisies.

As to myself, I have since had
much joy of London. My nights have been
as nights spent in the company of lovers.
I have played merry and yet have made
much good of myself. I am eighteen,
and have chattels and lace enough
by which a stranger might judge me a fine man.
I have a brace of snaphaunce from Tourner's,
and a sword all out of Damascene.

I do not think I will go home again.
God willing, I will make my home
hie to me as it were a good mare
coming up to the Bishop's Gate
and shaking her white head
at all the bells and carillons of London.

Gaia Holmes

Claustrophobia

On the morning bus
I can smell
a hundred lives
in the breath
that crowds the air;
old garlic, weak tea,
cornflakes, porridge.
The man sitting behind me
has the sap
of last night's woman
clinging to his beard,
relics of lust
gunking up the cracks
in his lips.
The office girl opposite
has the almond breath
of forced hunger
and rusty nail-head eyes
that wolf down
the passing hills.
The old woman beside me,
with a scab of jam
on her chin,
smells of raspberries
and loneliness,
I sniff wisps of grief
every time she moves.
There is the stable-scent
of a muesli breakfast
coming from the back,
hot straw and skimmed milk
pushed out by the heat vent.

Someone reeks of guilt,
like violets and sulphur,
like dentists gas
it makes me gag.
This invasion
of sweat, skin, soap
and stale love
is too intimate
for this time of day.
I press myself
against the window,
suck clean coldness
out of glass.

John Kinsella

Against Conflation

Designed to keep the parrots out
the Nissen hut of netting
trapped a pair of twenty-eights
vingt-huit, vingt-huit, vingt-huit,

a French colony, historic,
like the closing of brothels in Roe Street
or the surveillance
and vigilantes in Smith Street –

the new phoneboxes without
glass walls, citizens
with clipboard hoping
for kerb-crawlers, spitting

at streetwalkers – of refined varieties
in gardens that won't tolerate
trampling, the 'wandering about',
roughing it on the edge

of salinity, or in lingo,
making a go of it,
despite the gentrification,
the naming, the lists

bred from a new mathematics.
A storm struck hard
in the summer, and that's why
the netting lifted. The parrots'

panopticon of colours
looking for an out –
extra-spectra, safe in the open,
the daylight, their language.

Tim Liardet

The Language School

I

The charges might as well be read out
in Chinese, Bantu or Dravidian

or not be read at all – they drift, they loop
like light that cannot turn a corner

or soundwaves that bend in and out
of some fidelity to the original. To whom

do they cling? Another dumbstruck boy
who does not speak the English they speak

or even hear it – all nape and haircut, sat
folded up in a Jesuit clasp

with hands in his armpits, perusing
with a sort of thick-lipped composure

the platypus-nose of his left trainer, as if it had
evolved out of kilter with the rest.

II

No is the blank, the zero, the lumpy zilch,
the bijou fuck-all the question solicits

and wishes-for: the litany, the plural of no.
It is the answer the question anticipates

before asking itself, surrounding no.
Do you have anything to say in your own defence?

The hiatus, the answer-in-minus scans
the many milliseconds of a second

that hang like a threat, scaring it
way up into the corner of articulation

where it ceases to exist.
Without fuss, or noise, or anything,

without changing expression or looking up
the only yes there is nods to a no.

Andrew McNeillie

In Memoriam Carey Morris RA (1882–1968)

In the clutter of his studio
he made what I took to be trench tea,
leaves in the cup, hot water. No, Tommy
knew no such luxury, oh no...
But those leaves about my gums and teeth
made me gag as if a whiff of gas still
lingered on the air he breathed, enough to kill
a green recruit like me, or hasten death.

But death spared him then. He was a fighter,
this South Wales Borderer of the Slade
and Newlyn schools, a wheezy raconteur,
who told how Edward Thomas would call by,
sit where I sat, with that 'doomed look' he had,
as if already claimed for history.

Valeria Melchioretto

Cubism

Giovanni had mined 'Les Colline de l'Artois' for two years,
and was now ready to wash down the dust of his teens,
as rain washed the streets under that ugly, new Eiffel Tower.

In a bistro he heard himself order two glasses of red,
one for his throat and one for a man, who like him
spoke French as Frenchmen don't – unless they have got a cold.

After they couldn't count the empty glasses, no matter what language,
they made their way to his new friend's place, no 13 Rue Ravignan,
4th floor, 2nd door left after the steep stairs, and mind your head.

I don't know what the two discussed. Giovanni probably talked
about the pit, how even the largest mountain can be reduced
to briquettes, how each coal cube has the mountain's grotesque face.

Being a miner he knew all about cubism, because that's what he saw
when he walked the underground galleries with his lantern.
He could see a flickering mosaic of memories and rock.

The two men were kept awake by the biting blue winter
which Pablo painted for a living. He filled the stove with coal,
ripped a page from his sketch book and lit the fire.

That night they were both cold until a magenta sun rose
in Pablo's mind which ended the Blue Period. Years later
he would remember the tunnels of my grandfather's teens.

Peter Morgan

'Warum, Warum...?'

Somewhere a choir
is singing Brahms –
'Warum ist das Licht gegeben?'.

The light of summer
flickers through the leaves;
on through the window
to the window ledge

where one last crane-fly
steps his final dance –
rising on a rising note
to hammer hammer at the lamp

then fall in perfect pirouette –
to entrechat and strike his tone
of counterpoint, discordancy.

His act, an angered arabesque,
a double shuffle heel-and-toe;
the wrong dance to the wrong motet –
'Warum ist das Licht gegeben?'.

Outside the window
light is beaming light;
from leaf to ivy and to earth –
all green on green upon a green.

Inside the head, the heart, the house
such light cannot be dimmed or dulled
by right or wrongful miserere.

The crane-fly wails
his whine of lachrymalis;
batters one leg from the other,
batters anger at the brain.

I turn him out
with his embittered song
to dance his danse macabre
and sing his sad song to himself –

*'Warum ist das Licht gegeben...?
Warum ist das Licht?'.*

Togara Muzanenhamo

Captain of the Lighthouse

The late hour trickles to morning. The cattle low profusely by the
anthill
where brother and I climb and call Land's End. We are watchmen
overlooking a sea of hazel-acacia-green, over torrents of dust
whipping about
in whirlwinds and dirt tracks that reach us as firths.

We man our lighthouse – cattle as ships. We throw warning lights
whenever
they come too close to our jagged shore. The anthill, the orris-earth
lighthouse, from where we hurl stones like light in every direction.

Tafara stands on its summit speaking in *sea-talk*, Aye-aye me lad – a
ship's a-
coming! And hurls a rock at the cow sailing in. Her beefy hulk jolts
and turns.
Aye, Captain, another ship saved! I cry and furl my fingers into an
air-long
telescope – searching for more vessels in the day-night.

Now they low on the anthill, stranded in the dark. Their sonorous
cries haunt
through the night. Aye, methinks, me miss my brother, Captain of the
lighthouse, set sail from land's end into the deepest seventh sea.

Caitríona O'Reilly

A Qing Dish

Qianlong the stone-grinder stands to work at his trestle table.
His veins are paining. For years he has been grinding one piece of jade:
a white river boulder from the cold streams of Yarkand, in the West,
where wading river-girls find stones that flush to the temperature of
blood
at the touch of their numb footsoles and water-wrinkled hands.
What a skin it had... until the knife, loaded with toad-grease
and powdered almandine, bit deep enough to reveal an interior
of the most precious kind: the white of mutton-fat, clear and rare.

Qianlong is no sculptor. He can exhaust the jade only
with harder stones, with garnet, crushed emery or chips of ruby,
can only persuade it into patterns fit for an emperor's gaze.
He frowns. Behind him the wide plains are filled with ancestors' bones,
some disarranged in graves robbed of their stones, some in repose,
their tongue jades falling slowly through the osseous hoops of their
jaws.
Although he ignores the constellations spinning above him,
the Mongol winds that shape the hills circling his Yellow River home,

Qianlong knows something of all these. He is a kind of scholar.
He knows the bi disks, jade astrolabes, not for the heavens
(the stars have migrated like cranes since then) but for the serpents
surfacing on the jade's rivery skin. These he has learned,
with the sacred tiger, the cicada, the tinkling walls of Song vases.
He understands the lust of the fingers for small gems, beads
and amulets, the lips' desire to wear the stone thin with kissing.
His wife is worrisome. Lü Ta-Lin, his pupil, gives her lotus flowers.

Qianlong gives her jade combs for her hair. His assistants gather.
Now he mixes fine diamond dust into the grease and smears it
on the leathered end of his bamboo stick. Quickly, before the sun
brushes
the tips of the hills, Qianlong props his dish beside the window.
It is circular like the sun, its bevelled edges revealing, as petals,
a base in which two waxy catfish swim in and out of *lingzhi* scrolls.
When the sun declines, the dish is fired with a watery glaze like
celadon,
like light through ice or mist or paper, or the rarest of all whites,
nephrite.

Peter Reading

From -273.15

For I will consider my cat Tikka:
For she is an atheist;
For she does the eight rolly-polly in the mornings;
For this is the manner in which she *chooooses*
To express her gratitude and affection;
For she will leap upon the volumes
Heaped upon me by the *TLS* for review
And knock them all asunder
(This being an empirical demonstration
Of anarchy, and, to mention Lucretius,
Tantum religio potuit suadere malorum);
For she doth remark that 'In Egypt we was *Sacred* and all that';
For she doth consider how God is defunct;
For she can can-can, mew and chew biscuits and consider
How she and I and my wife are also defunct.

Jane Routh

The Red Cow

They were reaching north up the coast
for shelter in the lee of Skye, stiff with cold
after another day of stinging rain
and waves so short and steep they'd had to take
every sounding more than once,
when the last of the squalls raced away east
and a brief evening sun poured colour
back into the sea, so they all saw it: a cow
two cables off on the starboard quarter,
sitting on the waves and chewing a cud of tangle,
the curve of her spine and bony haunches
darker than a Hereford's, a rich red
among the *Glas Eileans* and the *Sgeir Dubhs* –
a single eccentricity in their meticulous work
and one unremarked by the Hydrographer.

Clare Shaw

Bird

Years ago, when I was young enough
to eat mud and be interested
in stones and clocks and buried bones –
when I was that young,
I found a bird that couldn't fly.
I picked it up. Its chest was flecked

like the surface of a road;
its wing was blackened straw; its eye
was a kind of corridor.
You can ignore the panic of wild things.
They struggle because
they don't know better.

I put it in a box and dug for worms;
uprooted the seedlings my father had grown
all winter in his steamy plastic frames.
They were thin green sinews, fragile as ice.
I broke them, and was shouted at of course,
and only three sore worms
and a damp gum of a slug to show for it.

And the bird wouldn't eat.
The far hole of its eye was misted over
like a sick cat or a
great-great-grandmother.
A distance, comfortless as a spider.
You couldn't touch or stroke it.
It would sink lower

beneath the hollow shoulders
and the eye would echo emptier.
The jamlid of water grew a skin of dust and feathers
and the food crawled and soured.
The bird smelt sick, like bad music.
Like something broken,

a thing done wrong.

But one day I woke
and what came from its throat
was a firework of sound that flowered,
that ran like a river
over stones where fish shimmer.
Quick otters swam in the dark of its song.
Clouds bloomed, sky grew suddenly tall

and the room was yellow with morning.
It was the third day.
The cardboard was soggy as bread.
The bird was all bones. By noon, it was dead.
What am I trying to say?
Nothing.
It just happened. It just happened like I said.

Ruth Silcock

The Perils of Ageing

Faster and faster the sledge travels over the snow,
Louder and louder the wolves are howling – we know
That we'll have to throw somebody out – and while the
    wolves feed
We can whip up the horses – our only hope is their speed.

But the night is still dark and the horses are tired and we hear
The distant howling of wolves once again coming near
And someone else must be thrown to the wolves – we all
    know
That soon it will be our turn to be flung on the snow.

Ivan Silverberg

The Equine Encounter

We are creeping
well after midnight
down through the dewy thicket,
our treads sounding
like shears through hair.
We carry apple peels
in the slack of our shirts.
The horses are kicking and hungry.
Predawn is black
and so crisp the shiest stars
cluster and come out,
the whole Milkyway streaking
the black of sky.
Andrea tells me
"We gotta move quick" in a warm
stir of breath.
The electric fence buzzes
and keeps us at bay,
but they stagger close,
their heads, great anvils,
and their lips, lambskin and gentle
as they eat skins from our palms,
cowering then coming
like cats searching our trust
figuring us out
with those poloping lips,

and us them
as the other end of the Earth
finally brims over the hills
and behind us, the Cowboy
buckling his belt and beating
his boots against the bars.
Andrea looks at me in the emerging day,
the stars still clustered in her eyes
knowing she would mount one of them
if urge came
and go like one from the sky.

Charles Tomlinson

The Portuguese Ox

was led by a woman –
a hand on each horn:
she, stepping backwards,
encouraged its advance,
her man between plough shafts
setting the course
where the rye had failed
and maize must grow now:
they stopped to talk
to us strangers at the granite wall and
with a loquacious pride
told over their possessions –
two tractors, a car, the land:
the beast stood there
like an interested listener,
patiently translating
inside its ox's brain
what was being said –
rather like me, as I
tried to penetrate their sibilant Portuguese:
it loomed in a silhouette
that resembled the statue of an ox,
but not for long, and when
it must move on once again
took up the tenor of its advance
in contrary motion, a slow
music, step by step
fading across that field
whose half-light hid
a terrain of scattered stones
autumn would submerge in grain.

Chase Twichell

Cocktail Music

All my life a brook of voices
has run in my ears,
many separate instruments
tuning and playing, tuning.
It's cocktail music,
the sound of my parents
in their thirties,
glass-lined ice bucket loaded
and reloaded but no one tending bar,
little paper napkins, cigarettes,
kids passing hors d'oeuvres.
It's drinking music,
riffle of water over stones,
ice in glasses, rise and fall
of many voices touching –
that music. Husbands grilling meat,
squirting the fire to keep it down,
a joke erupting, bird voices snipping
at something secret by the bar.
It's all the voices collapsed
into one voice,
urgent and muscled like a river,
then lowered, as in a drought,
but never gone. It's the background.
When I lift the shell to my ear,
it's in there.

Susan Utting

Woodwork

I'm building a box: not quick-assembled
with an Allen key and diagram, not pine
or MDF or even beech veneer, this one
is patina'd and grained in walnut,
dovetailed, countersunk and bevelled,
heavy-lidded, hinged with solid brass.

It's big: just big enough to hold
New York, a pilgrimage to Northern Spain,
a framed collage of cheapday travel cards
to castles; and a house with elbow-room
for two, sky windows and the sound
of Chinese wind chimes telling tales.

The picture of a person lying
at a crossroads will fit in beside
the sound his body made as it hit metal
and the way it trembled, bled along
with all the promises the morning
had just made about its afternoon.

The lid and body marry perfectly,
a soft click as the catch slips
into place – no need for chains
or padlocks; tap its sides and listen,
clench your fist and knock to hear
its low-pitched, empty echo.

A Van Jordan

From M.A.C.N.O.L.I.A.

Dr Wittenberg

In Service

Akron, Ohio, 1948

All of our neighbors are jealous:
MacNolia, with a mop
Or broom, a washboard or iron,
Is a magician.
Come over next week and bring
Some laundry – we'll show you
What she can do. She can spell
Any word you can pretty much
Think of; although – at least,
I'm not sure – I don't believe
She knows what they all mean.
They say she almost went to college.
Would you believe she wanted
To be a surgeon?
(She told us when she interviewed
To work here.) How could we say no?
But – lucky for us, I guess – she
Didn't get a scholarship.
Maybe she's saving up for her son
To go; I'll have to remember to ask.
She stays over on North St.
In a little home with her husband,
Who has some kind of off-and-on
Job, and they seem to do pretty well

For themselves with what she makes
Working in service here.
They say she
Spelled like a demon as a child.
They say she was almost
The national spelling champ, would've
Been the second one we had
From Akron in as little as three years...
I don't know, really, but I'm telling you –
She's the best damn maid in town.

after Marilyn Nelson

Jane Weir

Cigar

I must want it because
this is the third time this week.
You draw me out the way that salt
releases pent up sun from a tomato.
You take me through you, step by step.
When I'm not with you,
this is how you sit, how you swivel
your hips, stretch out your legs.
You lift my hand so it hovers
like a hummingbird over your nectar face.
You close your eyes. Sloth,
you ray my fingers, take two, press
them like Venetian glass to your bottom lip.
Drenched by my hair you whisper
into my ear as if speaking through
the intricate filigree of a grill.
I only have to think of you to see you.
I've heard this one before.
Snap. A swell inside my head,
a neap tide remembers again
as you come behind me,
a lantern slide and George Sand
is smoking her thin cigars.
She blows me words,
drowns me in a hoop-la
of Havana kisses.
Your eyes, grisly animal traps,
spring open and you're leading me

like a dancing bear to your desk,
that when I fool around with the lid,
before I sit on it, leaks the clawing
aroma of smoke, and I'm thinking
hold on don't take your jacket off,
I'm not ready – yet.

Hugo Williams

Walk Out to Winter

Are we dead, do you think? I thought we were
when I visited your art-school annexe
and saw your things all over the floor.
Someone had nailed a dress to a board
and thrown a pot of paint at it.
We left the flowers on your desk
and went for a walk near the reservoir.

The different sets of broken promises
lay in wait for us on the muddy path.
Alibis dragged themselves out of the mire.
What was I really doing last Friday?
Why didn't you leave a message about today?
Water hovered on the brink of ice
like an eye suddenly clouding over.

I remembered a book I had read once
which tells you what to do after you die:
stay calm, accept what has happened.
Then we went for a coffee in the Union Bar
and talked about our life together.
I watched from a great distance
as you lifted the cup to your lips.